5-MINUTE WRITING PROMPTS FOR KIDS

5-MINUTE WRITING PROMPTS FOR KIDS

FUN STORY STARTERS AND QUESTIONS TO
UNLEASH YOUR CREATIVITY

Chevahn Brown

Illustrated by Aditi Kakade Beaufrand

Z Kids · New York

Z Kids
An imprint of Zeitgeist™
A division of Penguin Random House LLC
1745 Broadway, New York, NY 10019
zeitgeistpublishing.com
penguinrandomhouse.com

ISBN: 9798217151332
Ebook ISBN: 9798217150960

Printed in the United States of America
2nd Printing

Illustrations by Aditi Kakade Beaufrand
Book design by Katy Brown
Author photograph © by Jaq Chen
Edited by Angelica Martinez

The authorized representative in the EU for product safety and compliance is Penguin Random House Ireland, Morrison Chambers, 32 Nassau Street, Dublin D02 YH68, Ireland.
https://eu-contact.penguin.ie

TO JAX AND NOLA,

YOU ARE THE STORIES

I'M MOST PROUD

OF CREATING.

CONTENTS

Introduction 8

How to Use This Book 10

FICTION
The Stories All Around You 12

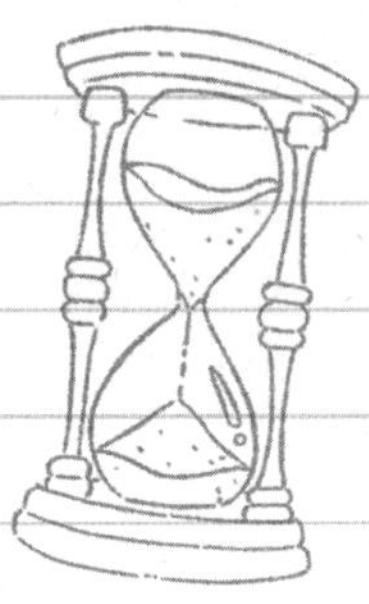

MYSTERY
Secrets, Puzzles, and Clues 32

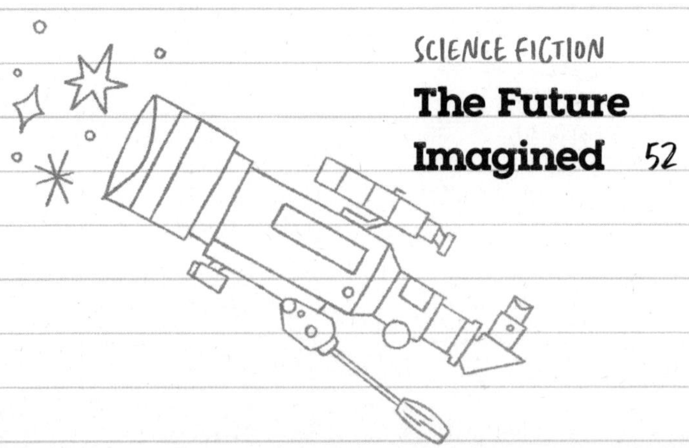

SCIENCE FICTION
The Future Imagined 52

FANTASY & ADVENTURE

The Hero's Journey 72

MEMOIR & AUTOBIOGRAPHY

The Story of You 94

Conclusion 111

Resources 113

Acknowledgments 115

Notes 119

Introduction

Welcome, young readers and writers-to-be! Did you know that anyone can be a writer? Yes, even you! The first step is to believe in your own curiosity and imagination. That tiny voice inside that asks, *What if?* Maybe you just finished a school project and found out how much fun writing can be, or perhaps you read a book that was so exciting you couldn't put it down. Maybe someone gave you this book because they knew you'd have fun with it. Whatever brought you here, get ready to take on the world of **creative writing**. Remember, every famous writer started somewhere.

In this book, you will find tons of imaginative **writing prompts**. Writing prompts are ideas that spark your imagination. Think of them as clues or questions. They act like the seed of a story, the concept that gets you writing. Some of the writing prompts include fun **twists**. Think of these twists as mini surprises that help open up the prompt and further develop the story idea.

This book of prompts is categorized by **genre.** The word *genre* describes the different types of style, mood, and content used to create a story. Think about the last few movies you watched or books you read. I bet they weren't all the same, right? Some may have been about magic and adventures. Maybe one was super funny, while another was scary or took place in the future with cool technology. These different kinds of stories are called genres! In this book, you'll write in the fiction, mystery, science fiction, fantasy and adventure, and memoir and autobiography genres.

I hope this book inspires you to think outside the box and find new ways to express yourself and your creativity. You will learn all sorts of things about your imagination, and you may even be surprised by the different characters, places, and stories you create! Just remember to have fun—it is the most crucial part of writing a story.

How to Use This Book

These creative writing prompts are like little sparks that help you come up with fun ideas for stories. Staring at a blank page can be intimidating! These prompts give you a starting point that then lets your imagination take over. From there, you get to take the wheel and decide just where your story will go.

There are a few ways to go through the book. Pick prompts at random, starting with your favorite genre, or go through the prompts in order, page by page. Choose the way that is most fun for you!

Aim to write for five minutes at a time for each prompt. Sometimes, you may feel like that isn't enough time, and sometimes getting to five minutes may seem challenging. If you end up going past five minutes, that's great—keep on writing for as long as you feel inspired! Either way, it's okay—the most important thing is to keep trying.

What you will need

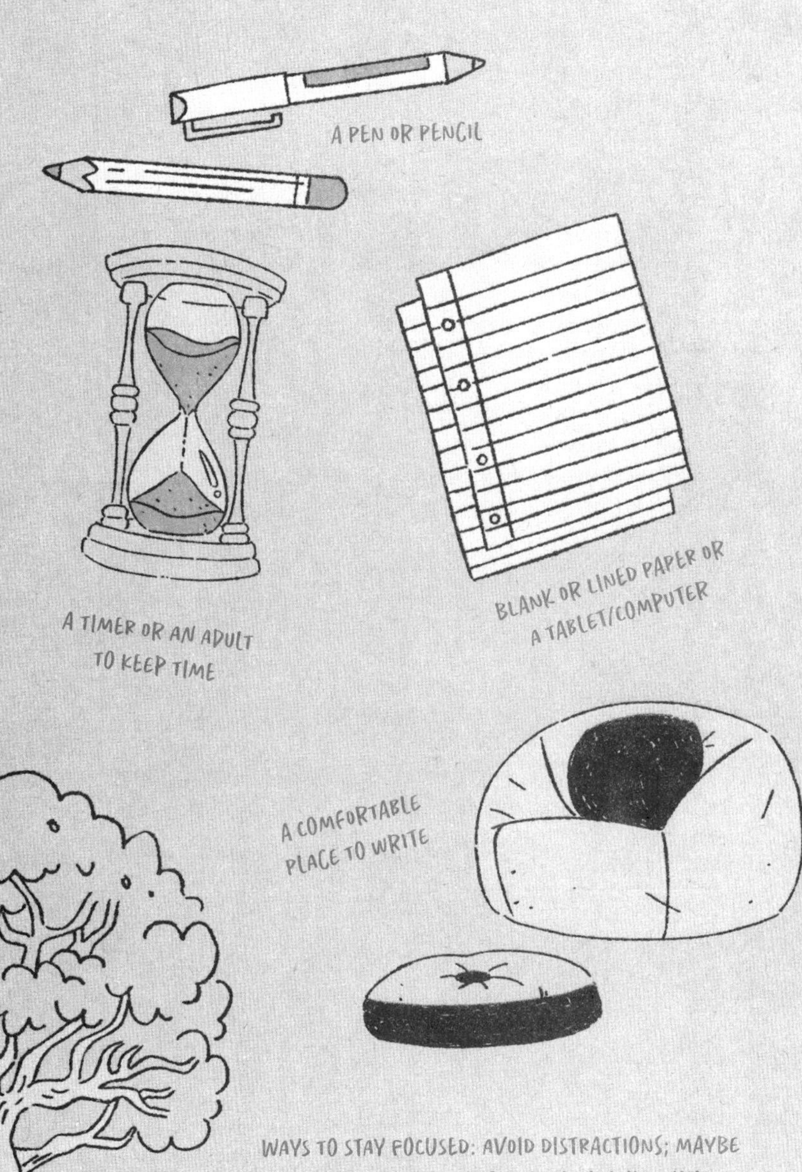

WAYS TO STAY FOCUSED: AVOID DISTRACTIONS; MAYBE SEEK OUT A QUIET PLACE, OR PLAY LIGHT MUSIC

FICTION

The Stories All Around You

Fiction is a genre where your imagination creates stories. These stories are set in realistic worlds, but the people, places, and events are not real.

For any book or story in fiction, the **characters**, **setting**, and **plot** are essential. The first step is to craft, or create, your main character, also known as a **protagonist**, by deciding what sort of person your story will focus on. The other characters are the other people in the story, such as friends, family members, or teachers. The setting is where the story takes place, like a town, school, or home. To create a good setting, consider where your main character would feel the most comfortable. The plot describes the sequence of events that make up the story. It has a beginning, a middle, and an end.

The best fiction books, or novels, are the ones where readers can learn from the characters' experiences. Writers invite the reader in by creating challenges and obstacles for the main character to experience. In the book-writing world, this is known as **conflict**. These are the actions that the main character experiences throughout the story. Conflict can be internal feelings, such as a main character worrying about riding a bike without training wheels. Conflict can also be external and come from someone called an **antagonist**. That is the person in your story who bothers or causes problems for the main character in some way. Like a classmate who always gets to the swings before you do at recess, even though they know it's your favorite thing to do! When you have all these parts in place, your story starts to come to life.

Whether it's navigating a tough friendship or embarking on a personal adventure, fiction opens up a world of experiences that feel close to home yet also leave room for the imagination.

WRITING TIPS

- Try to imagine as many details about your character as possible to bring them to life. What personality traits or quirks do they have? Are they chatty or shy? Do they collect things? Do they have specific fears or dreams?

- Your setting can create conflict and help move your story forward. Remember, try not to limit the story you're writing to your environment. Does your character live on a farm? Do they know the city streets well? What about a tree house—do they have one?

- Think of ways to make your obstacles be directly opposite of your main character's goals. For example, if your character dreams of impressing their school crush, then have their teacher unknowingly pair them up as partners for an important class project!

- Give your character different kinds of conflicts to encounter. You can use antagonists as obstacles in the form of another character, unusual happenings such as making a heavy mistake, or a big storm. Or you can use internal struggles, such as your protagonist's fear of letting someone down or their need to be right.

- Use dialogue to give readers a better idea of who your characters are. Provide them with different voices by changing the way they speak or having fun with word choice. You can even give each one their own unique quirks! For example, a character may have a trademark word or phrase they love to use, like "Oh boy!"

FICTION PROMPTS

Put five minutes on the clock. Ready. Set. Write!

1. **CONTINUE THE STORY:** I am walking home from school. A loud, screeching noise pierces my ears. The sound of metal crunching makes my heart race. I turn around and see . . .

2. Your parents tell you that you are moving to a new city tomorrow! You bike to your best friend's house to let them know. You've decided to complete your local bucket list now. Where do you start?

3. **CONTINUE THE STORY:** As I toss and turn in bed, I hear worried voices down the hall. My parents are whispering, but there is a third voice I don't recognize. My mouth drops open as I hear my mom say . . .

4. After school, one of the popular kids creates an exclusive club only for pretty people. They are so mean! You and your friends decide to make another group based on kindness. What do you do next to form your organization?

   TWIST: The next day, the president of the Pretty People Club asks to join yours. What do you do?

5. **CONTINUE THE STORY:** I'm staying with my family at a forest campground for a week. The family in the tent next to ours has a kid my age. They're playing with an oddly shaped box. I walk up to them and . . .

TWIST: Soon, you team up together. What new adventures do you get into?

6. One morning, a surprise visitor rings your doorbell with important information for your family. What do they share?

TWIST: You notice something odd about the visitor. What is it?

7. While searching for a lost item in the basement, you find old photos of your parents wearing fancy clothing. You almost don't recognize them! What else do you learn about them?

8. **CONTINUE THE STORY:** During class, the power goes out, and everyone starts to panic. The teacher has an idea to calm us down, so we begin to . . .

TWIST: The principal announces over the intercom that everyone must go to the gym immediately. What happens there?

9. When you get to school, your teacher is absent, and a substitute says they have a special project for the whole class. What is it?

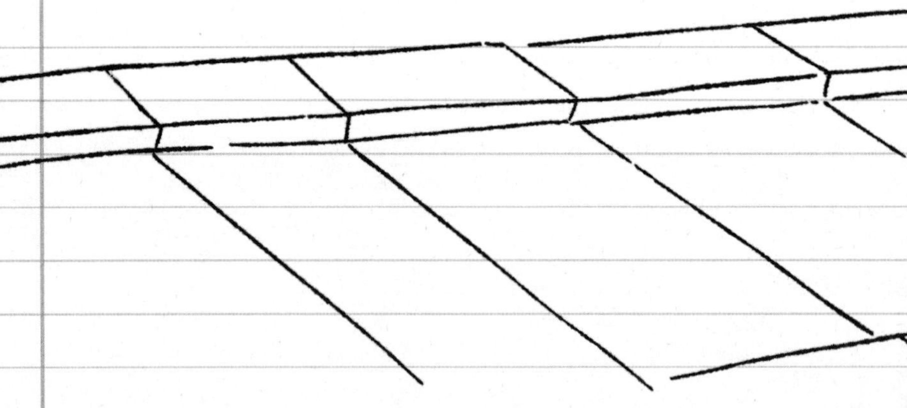

10. **CONTINUE THE STORY:** I'm walking home from school when I notice a shiny, beautifully wrapped gift box on the sidewalk. I look around to see if someone has dropped it, but the street is empty. When I inspect it, I see my name on the tag and I . . .

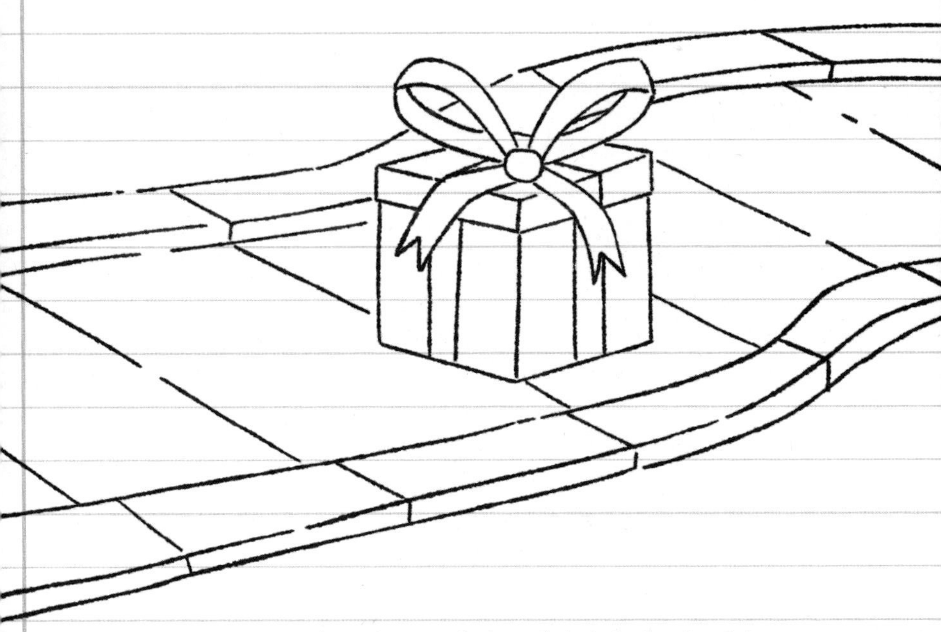

11. For the past few weeks, you've been working on a science project with the school bully. They bring such negative energy, and you feel like you can't take it anymore. Today, they push your part of the project off the desk, shattering glass everywhere. What do you do?

12. You've decided to be a volunteer librarian for the day. What's the first thing you do?

13. At summer camp last year, you pinkie promised your friend that you would always bunk together. When you return to camp this year with your neighborhood best friend, you've completely forgotten about your promise, but your camp friend hasn't forgotten at all. What do you do?

14. **CONTINUE THE STORY:** It's Saturday morning, and my basketball team is warming up for a game. It's the last game before finals, and I've trained harder than usual. Suddenly, our team's star player twists their ankle, and the coach looks to me to step in for them. I . . .

15. You're trying to surprise your good friend for their birthday. It's hard, though, because they're always with you! How do you figure out a way to distract them or keep them busy so that the surprise isn't ruined?

16. **CONTINUE THE STORY:** It's Sunday morning, and I've slept in. I know it's later than usual because I don't hear my dad blaring the sports channel or my mom cooking breakfast. I don't hear anything at all. So I . . .

TWIST: Your parents' cars are still in the garage, and everything is left as it was the night before, completely untouched. Where do you go next?

17. A big storm that can destroy entire buildings is headed directly to your town. How do you and your family prepare for it?

18. There is a new student in your class today, and your teacher seats them next to you. You are their first-day buddy. What do you show them first, second, third . . . ?

TWIST: What if English isn't their first language?

19. Your parents force you to tag along with your older sister when she's out with friends. What do you do, and what do you learn about her?

20. **CONTINUE THE STORY:** My best friend lives just a few houses down from me. We do everything together! One day, her friend from where she used to live visits. She seems jealous that we are now best friends. She doesn't want me to go to the movies with them that night. So I . . .

21. You receive a special invitation for a fancy party in the mail, but you have no idea who it's from. You decide to go anyway. At the party, everyone seems to know you, but you've never heard of any of them, so you . . .

    TWIST: Finally, you see someone you recognize. What do they tell you?

22. You're hanging out in your front yard, kicking a ball, when you notice the neighbor across the street has a new dog. Out of the blue, the dog takes off down the street! What do you do next?

23. **CONTINUE THE STORY:** When I get to school, I find a note on my desk. It has a heart drawn on the top. I open it, and it says . . .

24. **CONTINUE THE STORY:** One summer day, my friend and I discovered a message in a bottle that had washed ashore. My friend read the message out loud. A child wrote the letter almost a hundred years ago! I searched the child's name online and found out that . . .

25. **CONTINUE THE STORY:** I'm hiking through a challenging trail with a few friends. Suddenly, we hear a low growl from the woods. A small wolf approaches with snarling teeth. We try not to panic, but . . .

    TWIST: You remember that you recently read something about wolves, so you try your luck and be brave by . . .

26. Your school is putting on a play, and you're excited about your role. You've been practicing your lines for weeks. What character are you playing, and what are they like?

27. CONTINUE THE STORY: My family is out for dinner. The restaurant is cold, and I forgot my sweater in the car. I go to the car to get it, and on my way back to the restaurant, I pass by a dark alley and hear something whimpering. I find a wounded animal and decide to . . .

28. There is an old dirt road near your house that you've never walked on before because it goes up into the hills. One summer day, you decide to walk the trail. What do you find?

29. You head to the bathroom in the middle of class. You turn the corner to a long hallway and see a pair of feet jutting out from another classroom's door. You approach them and realize someone has passed out. What do you do?

30. You and your friends are going for a dip in the local creek. You all take turns jumping in. After one of them jumps, you hear sharp yelling. Your friend has twisted their ankle on a rock. What do you do?

TWIST: What if the injury is so bad that your friend can't walk on it? How do you help them?

MYSTERY

Secrets, Puzzles, and Clues

If you enjoy solving riddles and puzzles or investigating crimes and unexpected situations, then the **mystery** genre might be perfect for you! Mystery stories have suspense, thrills, twists, and surprises. **Suspense** is the feeling of sitting on the edge of your seat. Mysteries build suspense by leaving some **clues**, or hints, for readers while withholding others. These stories are meant to engage the reader and put them in the **detective seat**. In that way, the story usually follows a curious protagonist, who may be a detective, as they try to solve a puzzling scenario. Often, clues tell the reader what's to come, also known as **foreshadowing**.

A mystery might follow a map leading to an unusual treasure, or it could be about watching a suspicious new neighbor. Along the way, your character may face suspects, challenges, dangers, and unexpected twists before finally arriving at the answer. Whichever path your story takes, it will surely include strange events or situations that are difficult to explain without further investigation.

When you set out to write a mystery, a good place to start is with an interesting question like, What happened here? Who came by during that time? Why?

Are you ready to write your story? Let's get started uncovering secrets!

WRITING TIPS

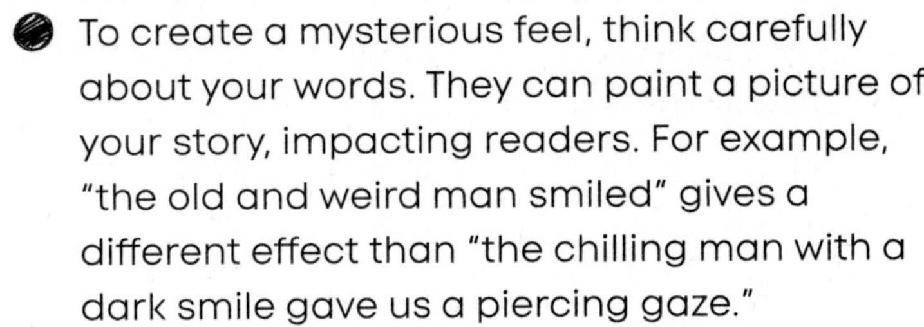

- To create a mysterious feel, think carefully about your words. They can paint a picture of your story, impacting readers. For example, "the old and weird man smiled" gives a different effect than "the chilling man with a dark smile gave us a piercing gaze."

- Knowing exactly where the investigation will end up can help. It also makes it easier to leave clues along the way that hint at what's to come.

- As you write the story, think about what your reader already knows through the information you've left as clues and what is left to share with the reader. That way, you can track how much of the puzzle has been revealed.

- One way to create interesting characters is to make them complex. That means that the reader isn't sure if they are good or bad. Show us details about the characters that portray them as potentially sinister or innocent.

- To write a fun twist, first know where your story is headed. Then think of an alternative ending or a surprise to fool the readers along the way. That way, when your real ending is played out, the readers will be surprised!

MYSTERY PROMPTS

Put five minutes on the clock. Ready. Set. Write!

31. The book you checked out of the library has a bizarre code written in pen on the last page. You and your friend finally cracked the code. What did it say?

32. **CONTINUE THE STORY:** For the past few nights, I have heard a strange noise coming from the next-door neighbor's house. It doesn't sound like a pet, so I'm going to investigate the source of the sound. I start by sneaking across the grass, where I find . . .

    TWIST: As you're investigating, a light turns on inside your neighbor's house. What do you do next?

33. **CONTINUE THE STORY:** When I arrived at school this morning, everyone was surprised to see that the doors were still locked. The janitorial staff was missing their keys. I overheard the teachers talking about . . .

34. You notice a flock of birds circling over your neighborhood lake—this never happens! As the flock grows larger, you sneak over to the lake to see what the commotion is about. What do you find?

35. You're packing up your backpack at the end of the day, and you notice a note sticking out of its side pocket. It reads "Your backyard, 8 p.m. Don't be late. You know who this is." What do you do?

TWIST: Your best friend got the same note. What do you do?

36. Today, your class has a visitor: a real detective who is talking about their work. The detective has to step out to take an emergency call. You raise your hand for the bathroom, and as you walk down the hall, you eavesdrop on the detective's call. What do you hear?

37. Your dad owns an authentic Samurai sword, which his former boss gave him. No one is allowed to touch it, but he always shows it off. One night, you walk by his office and see his window is open. The sword is missing! What do you do?

TWIST: The next day, you hear someone at school talking about this cool new Samurai sword their big brother got them. What do you do?

38. Day after day, you notice that different equipment is going missing from your school science lab. No one thinks there's anything sinister about it until you and your best friend see the lab closet door ajar one day after school. What do you find?

39. CONTINUE THE STORY: After school, I like to hang out by the big oak tree to write in my journal or read a book. One day, I see someone put something in the large tree's hollow. I ignore it this time, but the next day, there are more items in there. I decide to take a peek and . . .

40. **CONTINUE THE STORY:** As I'm falling asleep, I get an odd text that reads "Cassandra, I know you're there. I need help!" That's not my name, but I reply. It turns out the person on the other end is stuck in a . . .

TWIST: Following a GPS tracker from the person in need, you are led to a building with a time machine. What do you do?

41. **CONTINUE THE STORY:** My friends and I are kicking a ball around a park when I notice a shadowy figure lurking by some trees. I have a weird feeling about it, but when our ball rolls into the trees, we discover that the shadowy figure is actually a dog that is . . .

42. Your best friend takes you aside before school and tells you a secret about one of your classmates. You agree to meet after school to investigate, but by the afternoon, mysteriously, no one has seen your friend at all. What do you do?

43. You are doing your best to follow your chore list, and the next step is cleaning the doghouse. When you get inside the small wooden house, you see that your dog has been collecting random keys of all shapes and sizes. What do you do next?

44. CONTINUE THE STORY: My friend and I are bored, so we follow our town's only train tracks to see where they go. No one's ever seen a train go by, so we are sure it's safe to walk on the tracks. After walking for some time, we come upon an old-school steam train that seems to have no conductor. It . . .

TWIST: Your friend is way too scared to investigate. They turn to run away and trip over the tracks. When they do, the steam train blares out a deafening horn. What do you do?

45. **CONTINUE THE STORY:** My brother and I are removing a few items from the attic so our parents can do some spring cleaning. We find a letter wedged between some old books. The letter is dated 1878 and mentions a puzzle that needs to be figured out. We . . .

TWIST: Your mom thinks it belonged to your great-great-grandmother, who witnessed a well-known crime and went into hiding to keep safe. How does this information help you solve the puzzle?

46. **CONTINUE THE STORY:** One of my basketball teammates always disappears for 15 minutes during each game. It's frustrating because we depend on him! One day, I followed him when he left. He headed out the back door of the gym and . . .

47. New neighbors are moving into the house across the street. One day, you see a moving truck outside the house, but no people. Each day, it looks like the house is more lived in, yet you've never seen a soul. How are they going unseen?

48. Your father asks you to get something from the basement, and you notice muddy footprints tracking across the floor. The footprints start at a cracked window. Where do they lead?

49. **CONTINUE THE STORY:** My parents are watching the news before school, and I hear that the school librarian has gone missing. On my walk to school that day, I swear I see the librarian's face in one of the windows of a bus that drives past me. I . . .

50. Overnight, a thick fog settled over your town, making it difficult to see directly ahead of you. Officials caution you to stay indoors, but you venture down the road to see your friend. Something emerges from the fog. What is it?

51. **CONTINUE THE STORY:** It's my 13th birthday, and my parents give me an old diary that belonged to my dad's grandfather. He made them promise not to open it and to only give it to me on this specific birthday. I open it in private and read instructions from my grandfather telling me to . . .

52. You're staring out the window while taking a class test, racking your brain for answers. Afterward, one of your friends is accused of cheating. You know that he didn't because you kept staring in his direction. How can you prove his innocence?

53. Your class takes a field trip to the local history museum. You see a painting by an unknown artist, but you notice a familiar inscription in the bottom right corner. You've seen this inscription before on a painting in your grandfather's office. What do you do next?

TWIST: When you go see Grandpa on the weekend, you take another look at the painting. What's odd about it?

54. You're throwing a basketball against your bedroom wall. It's an old house, but you never expected the ball to accidentally damage the wall. When you inspect further, pulling the crumbling drywall away, you see that there is a hidden door. What do you do?

55. **CONTINUE THE STORY:** My family is vacationing on a tropical island. As I head toward a shaded area of palm trees, I see something glinting behind some rocks. I find an old compass peeking out from the rubble. The compass doesn't point north, but it is pointing . . .

TWIST: After following the compass for some time, you notice it is directing you toward some caves. What do you do next?

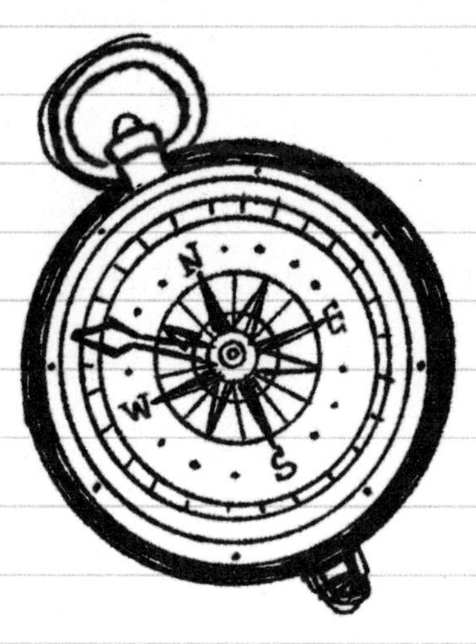

56. **CONTINUE THE STORY:** My school has a terrible problem with graffiti. A group of kids is tagging different areas of the school. At first, the graffiti seemed like nonsense, but then I discovered a connection. It is spelling out . . .

57. **CONTINUE THE STORY:** I've been seeing more and more Missing Dog signs going up. I'm worried about what's happening to the dogs in town. One night, as I'm walking my pup, I hear a deep growling coming from down the street and . . .

    TWIST: When you jog ahead to see what's happening, you see bloody paw prints trotting into the darkness. With a gulp, you hold your dog's leash tighter. What do you do?

58. During your town's homecoming football game, the cheerleaders rush onto the field for a halftime performance. You notice the mascot, a grizzly bear, stumbling out of the locker room toward the field. No one else sees the bear clutching its stomach and falling to the ground. What do you do?

59. You and your friend always attend the same summer camp for a week. On beach day, you wander farther than you're allowed. That's when you come upon an abandoned sailboat, flipped over in the sand. What do you find near the boat?

60. **CONTINUE THE STORY:** The principal announces that someone is stealing hall passes from the office. At lunch, you see many of them in your friend's backpack. You . . .

SCIENCE FICTION

The Future Imagined

Do you dream of coming up with new inventions, visiting another planet, or time traveling to the future or past? If so, you're already thinking like a **science fiction** writer! Also called **sci-fi**, this genre takes readers beyond the limits of the real world. They involve realities different from our own with futuristic technology, strange new planets, and incredible possibilities. As robots and artificial intelligence become more powerful, humans can explore the galaxy without constraints. Sci-fi also asks big **what-if** questions. What if we could talk to aliens? What if we could read other minds? What if machines become smarter than people?

Science fiction uses ideas from real discoveries and theories. Some stories take place in the far future, while others show a world much like ours but with a twist—like a hidden portal to another dimension! Writers use key sci-fi elements, such as **advanced technology**, **space exploration**, **time travel**, and **artificial intelligence**, to build exciting worlds.

Ready to travel along your imagination? Grab your thinking cap and prepare to blast off into the science fiction universe!

WRITING TIPS

- One way to come up with a new invention is to observe the world around you and try to think of the things your school or town needs. What are some ideas that could improve your life?

- Think about how things are usually done and then add a scientific twist. For example, houses and buildings run on electricity, but what if they ran on some other type of energy, like juice or rain?

- Think of how to change your reality in little ways—for example, a city that sleeps during the day, or roads that disappear. Sometimes, a silly sci-fi reality is only slightly different from our normal reality!

- Try to keep your conflicts centered on your sci-fi elements. For example, if you're using time travel, try having obstacles arise from the mechanism. Some part of the device could break or a wonky setting could cause a time-travel catastrophe! Be sure not to leave your sci-fi elements in the background; make them the main part of your story!

- Be sure to think through each sci-fi element you use. If there is a new machine, give it a name! Detail what it looks like. You can even make up new materials to describe what it's made of.

SCI-FI PROMPTS

Put five minutes on the clock. Ready. Set. Write!

61. Before your grandmother died, she gave you an old pair of glasses. When you finally put them on, you realize that you can see people making decisions, their alternate realities flowing out of them like glowing movies. Do you tell anyone? How do your adventures unfold?

62. **CONTINUE THE STORY:** I'm up in the attic and come across an old mirror that shows me from the future! My reflection tells me that my older self is in danger, and I need to . . .

63. You head into your classroom on a normal morning. When you sit at your desk, though, you notice that the person in front of you seems to have a blue blinking light peeking out from beneath their skin. What do you do?

TWIST: They start to realize that you're onto them. They gather their belongings and dash outside, so you follow them! What's waiting for you outside?

64. **CONTINUE THE STORY:** My teacher has assigned our class an exciting project. Everyone is to take home an egg, place it in water, and watch as the shell dissolves, revealing a hidden fossil. When my egg hatches, a little purple webbed foot pokes out and . . .

65. **CONTINUE THE STORY:** My best friend got a cool new virtual reality headset for their birthday, so they asked me to come over and try it out. Inside the virtual game, the first thing I see is . . .

TWIST: When you and your friend try to exit the game and take the headset off, you realize you can't. You're trapped! What do you do next?

66. **CONTINUE THE STORY:** I'm up late on my phone, and my mom gives me my final warning: "It's bedtime. No more screens!" I set my phone down and close my eyes. But then I hear a grainy voice in the dark ask, "Are you there?" My phone lights up; it's talking to me! I . . .

67. One morning, you wake up, trip over your orange kitten, and stub your toe. The rest of the day continues as usual. The next day, you wake up, trip over your kitten again, and stub your toe. As the day continues, you realize you're living the same day twice! What do you do?

68. **CONTINUE THE STORY:** In the middle of the night, I wake up to go to the bathroom, but my legs feel wobbly. When I look out the window, I see that my house is floating through the air. So I grab . . .

TWIST: Once your town is far below, you wake up your sibling. What do they say?

69. **CONTINUE THE STORY:** My dog and I are playing fetch in the backyard, and the ball rolls into the woods. When we go look for it, we see a strange sight: a young boy who says he's from the future. He's lost and needs my help! I . . .

TWIST: He begins speaking in an unknown language and points to an interesting gadget on his wrist. What does it do?

70. CONTINUE THE STORY: Our class is on a field trip to a local space station. My friend and I accidentally get separated from our group. As we try to find our way back, I stumble upon a room with white smoke coming from underneath the door and . . .

71. **CONTINUE THE STORY:** One day after school, another student and I are the last people to be picked up. Bored, we wander through the gym looking for something to do. We're heading into the closet to get some dodgeballs when we see something glowing in the back. A secret cabinet that . . .

72. Your science teacher allows your class to pass around a meteorite donated to the school. After class, you hang back to steal another glance. Now the meteorite is glowing and cracking open. What do you do?

73. **CONTINUE THE STORY:** My brother and I are attempting an at-home experiment using directions from YouTube. We accidentally mix up one of the ingredients. When the mixture gets on our hands, my brother and I start shrinking. We . . .

74. For the past month, your writing class has been exploring letter writing through pen pals. In your pen pal's most recent letter, they tell you they are not actually from this planet. They sent you something in an envelope from their planet. What is it?

75. In a futuristic world, pet animals have been banned and replaced with robot dogs and cats. How do they act? How can people tell the difference between real and robotic pets?

76. CONTINUE THE STORY: My science teacher has a brand-new experiment for our class, but it won't be ready until the afternoon. I'm too impatient and sneak into the classroom during lunch to see what's inside. Walking toward a big box, I hear a rumbling growl from within and . . .

77. CONTINUE THE STORY: I'm stargazing in my backyard with my sister's new telescope. The moon is so beautiful. Then, all of a sudden, we see flashing lights from the surface. It seems like it's communicating by Morse code. It says . . .

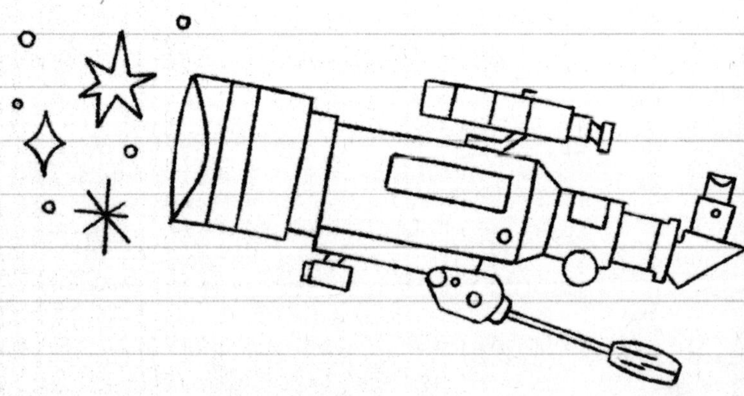

78. Your family has recently adopted a puppy. He is very cute but seems a bit quiet and down. One night, you peer into his eyes and tell him, "Everything's okay; you're safe here." The puppy then reveals its secret powers. What can the puppy do?

TWIST: Your puppy finds a way to jump out your window, and you have to get him back before anyone sees him! What do you do?

79. **CONTINUE THE STORY:** My parents got me the toy robot I wanted for my birthday. The robot helps me with chores and other tasks around the house—it's fun! One day, I see the robot digging around in my parents' office and . . .

80. CONTINUE THE STORY: After playing at the park with friends, I ride my bike home in the rain to try to beat the storm. Suddenly, thunder rumbles and lightning strikes and knocks me off my bike! I can see electricity buzzing all over my skin and . . .

TWIST: The sparks of electricity have given you special powers. What has changed about you?

81. You hear weird sounds coming from your dad's office. There, you find a beeping machine with instructions on it. The machine asks you to place a strand of hair on it, and it uses the strand to create a clone of you! What is the first thing you do?

82. **CONTINUE THE STORY:** A new technology allows people to travel through time. As one of the lucky winners of a giveaway contest, I get to try out the tech! I place the small device on the side of my head, and suddenly . . .

83. **CONTINUE THE STORY:** An old factory in our small town has gone awry, causing various odd changes. All the changes seem manageable until one day, gravity disappears. Everything around me begins to float up and . . .

84. You have an eerie feeling that someone is watching you in your backyard, so you set up a trap to catch them. When the device is triggered, you notice it's not just someone—it's something! What is it?

TWIST: The creature is observing you and wants to know how humans communicate. What do you say?

85. **CONTINUE THE STORY:** I am exploring an abandoned spaceship at the science museum when I find a hidden hatch. Inside, I press a button that brings the ship to life and locks me in. The next thing I know, the ship is taking off and . . .

TWIST: You find a control board filled with colorful, beeping buttons. You have to figure out how to operate this thing to avoid crashing. How do you save the ship?

86. What would happen if you woke up in a world where the power structure has been changed? Kids are now in charge of adults. What would be the first thing you do?

87. One day at science camp, you are meeting with your science mentor. He steps outside for just a moment, and you find a mysterious hat glowing in the corner. When you put it on, it allows you to become invisible! What do you do next?

88. **CONTINUE THE STORY:** One morning, I wake up to find all my apps missing from my phone. Only one mysterious app remains, and I've never seen it before. When I tap into it, a message plays from someone who lives in another galaxy. It says . . .

89. **CONTINUE THE STORY:** Scientists have figured out how to harness the energy of joy, play, and amusement using a wearable device. They now use this energy to fuel the world, and . . .

TWIST: To make sure the world never runs out of fuel, society has now completely banned all work and instead encourages only playing. What happens when humans are forced to have fun? What problems could arise from this world?

90. You're a pretty serious gamer who breaks through a new level in a game. Suddenly, your avatar steps out of the screen. It materializes into a hologram before your eyes. Your avatar looks and acts like you but is crazy strong! What do you do next?

FANTASY AND ADVENTURE

The Hero's Journey

Imagine you are soaring through the skies on the back of a dragon or defending a magical kingdom by defeating an evil creature. When you start thinking outside your everyday world and using your imagination to dream up a mythical and exciting world, you're acting like a fantasy writer! **Fantasy** and **adventure** stories take readers on incredible journeys beyond the real world, where anything is possible. You might use some fantastical tropes, such as talking animals, daring quests, enchanted forests, and secret maps.

In this genre, you'll find some common elements that make stories exciting and wonderful. **Magical worlds** are at the heart of many fantasy stories. These can be completely different from

our world, like a land with floating islands or one filled with mythical creatures. You might also find **fantastical creatures**, like dragons, unicorns, or talking animals, which add mystery and excitement to the story.

Heroes and **heroines** are a big part of the adventure. They might be ordinary kids who discover they have extraordinary abilities, or they could be brave knights or clever wizards on essential quests. Of course, there are villains, too—evil sorcerers, dark forces, or even tricky creatures who try to stop the heroes from completing their mission.

Adventure and **exploration** are key in fantasy. Characters might journey through unknown lands, solve ancient riddles, or battle fearsome foes. But beyond the action, fantasy stories also explore big themes like bravery, friendship, loyalty, and the choice between good and evil.

Are you feeling adventurous yet? Let's grab your imagination like a sword, pack your ideas like a treasure map, and prepare to create a world only you can dream up! The possibilities are endless in fantasy and adventure.

WRITING TIPS

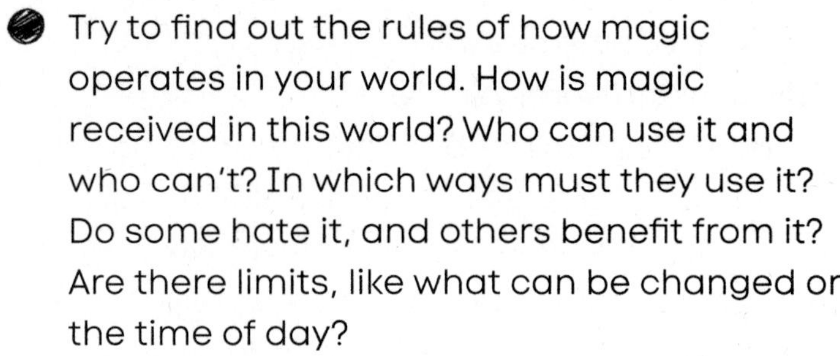

- Try to find out the rules of how magic operates in your world. How is magic received in this world? Who can use it and who can't? In which ways must they use it? Do some hate it, and others benefit from it? Are there limits, like what can be changed or the time of day?

- Create a unique setting. What do the buildings look like, and how do they differ from the ones in your world? Can all creatures in this new world talk, think, and feel?

- Give your protagonist a specific or adventurous journey within their magical world. Are they hoping to pass an initiation, prove their value to an elder, or discover for themselves what lies within?

- Create a conflict for your protagonist. For example, your protagonist is a dragon who avoids combat. How would this make the story more dramatic?

- Change the expectations and keep readers guessing. We've read about mermaids, fairies, and dragons before, but try to tweak your story to break it out of the mold. For example, perhaps the fairies in your story can't fly, but they can swim!

FANTASY PROMPTS

Put five minutes on the clock. Ready. Set. Write!

91. Your family is staying at a remote cabin for the weekend. You stumble upon a hidden pond in the woods behind the property. Suddenly, a fish pops out of the water—it can talk! What does it say?

92. You are tired of always being the youngest. One day, you wake up and realize you've switched bodies with your older sibling. Instead of going to school today, you find yourself going to work as your sibling. Everyone believes you are an adult. What is the first thing you do?

    TWIST: At your older sibling's job, their boss wants to talk to you about a promotion! What do you do?

93. **CONTINUE THE STORY:** One hot summer day, I stopped by the local lake to cool off with friends. I noticed metallic scales bobbing on the surface. It looked like a baby dragon. I . . .

94. In the art supply room at school, you discover a sparkling door hidden by a stack of paint. You take a deep breath and open it. On the other side, you find a world entirely made of plants—plant homes, plant people, plant food. What's the first thing you do?

    TWIST: You find that certain large plants are aggressive enemies. How do you fight them off?

95. You wake up feeling groggy, like you've slept for 50 hours. Your hand immediately notices something cold and metal underneath your pillow. It's a golden key with writing on it that reads "Unlocks your greatest dreams." Where do you head first?

96. You find a handwritten letter in your mailbox addressed to you. It's sending you on a quest to rescue a missing puppy. The only rule is that your one companion is already chosen for you: the one student in class you don't like very much. How do you approach them?

TWIST: It turns out it'll take all afternoon, so how do you explain to your parents that you won't be home after school until dinnertime?

97. CONTINUE THE STORY: One night during summer camp, my friend and I walk into the woods. We see a wolf and freeze. But instead of chasing us, it bows and wants us to . . .

TWIST: When you two approach the wolf, you notice a glowing pendant around its neck. What is on the pendant?

98. **CONTINUE THE STORY:** One day in the middle of class, a little green creature climbs out of my phone and starts speaking to me, but no one else can see it. It . . .

99. Your family stays at your grandparents' beach house during the holidays. One night, you and your sister see an island not too far from shore, illuminated by the full moon. You've never seen it before. The next day, it is gone, only to return under the moonlight that night. How do you investigate?

100. When you step outside, the world is bleak and gray. Everything is black and white, with only a spectrum of gray to highlight differences. It turns out a villain has stolen all the colors from your reality. What do you do?

TWIST: You find a footprint trail of color and track it down in hopes of finding the villain. Instead, what do you see?

101. CONTINUE THE STORY: I walk past my sibling's bedroom, and I see a pair of huge eyes peering in through the window. A large smile follows me. I tiptoe over to the window and see a giant squatting down and facing me. They know my name and hand me a . . .

102. CONTINUE THE STORY: It's daylight saving time today. My parents have asked me to change the clocks around the house. In their office, an old clock is hard to budge. Finally, I manage to turn the dial, and then I see the sun rise higher in the sky. It turns out this clock can change time, and . . .

103. Your parents have been keeping chickens for the past six months, and you've started growing attached to them. One morning, as you are retrieving some eggs, you notice that one of the eggs is glowing. What hatches out of it?

TWIST: That night, the entire henhouse starts to glow. What do you and your family find out?

104. You've been sick. Nothing serious, just a cold that is taking forever to go away! Your mom's friend comes by with a homemade tea. You agree to try it, and that's when she shares the one side effect. What is it?

105. **CONTINUE THE STORY:** I'm reading the latest fantasy novel I've checked out from the library. The story grips me with every word. One night, as I'm reading, I'm pulled directly into the book and find myself in the middle of . . .

TWIST: What happens when one of the characters realizes you are not from their world?

106. You wake up with a mysterious case of hiccups that won't go away. It isn't until you encounter your little brother that you realize your hiccups are contagious. Not only that, but you seem to be spreading some sort of magical powers with every hiccup. What are the powers?

107. You wake up to find an hourglass with tiny grains of sand slowly slipping through placed on your dresser. It comes with a note that reads "Find the wizard before it's too late." You notice a trail of sand that leads from the dresser to your open window. What do you do next?

108. A golden feather floats down from your backyard tree. That's when you notice a large golden phoenix, its wings on fire, soaring above. All around your town, dozens of phoenixes are taking over and accidentally burning down buildings. How can you stop them?

TWIST: One of the phoenixes swoops down and tells you that an evil force has taken over their world, which is why they are now appearing in your world. How can you help?

109. An old tree with a massive trunk stands tall in your local park. One day, while you're reading by the tree, you hear whispers in the wind. As the leaves shake, quiet secrets come tumbling down. You close your book and listen in. What secrets does the tree share?

110. You and your best friend have been made aware of a lost magical scroll. You learn that it can grant wishes. You two must use your rock-climbing skills to try to climb an incredibly tall mountain to find it. What happens when one of you gets hurt?

111. **CONTINUE THE STORY:** I've found a hidden city deep underground in my hometown, but everything is frozen solid. Something must have happened to freeze the town. All of a sudden, I hear ice breaking. Something is thawing and . . .

112. Breaking news blares from your television one morning. Your family listens in as they learn about a powerful curse that is spreading across the nation. The curse causes everyone to fall into a deep sleep. How do you stop it before it reaches your town?

113. One hot summer night, you and your neighbor are stargazing with your new telescope. You are amazed to find that the stars are forming a message in the sky. Each night, a bit more of the message is revealed to you. What does it end up saying?

114. CONTINUE THE STORY: I wake up and get out of bed, only to fall through a portal. I'm racing through the sky, clouds all around me. That's when I notice that my arms are growing feathers. In this world, everything has wings and . . .

115. **CONTINUE THE STORY:** I'm studying for a test at the library when I hear a whisper next to me. No one is there. I focus on my studying, but then I hear the whispering again. This time, I see the outline of a childlike ghostly figure. It needs me to . . .

TWIST: After you help the child, they ask if they can stay the night at your house. How do you let them in and make sure no one else realizes they are there?

116. **CONTINUE THE STORY:** One day, after a misty, hot rainstorm, my best friend notices a large rainbow blanketing the sky. The two of us decide to chase the rainbow to find its end. We are shocked to find . . .

117. **CONTINUE THE STORY:** I'm on a class field trip at an abandoned castle from the 1600s. I hear music playing from another room and find an ancient record player, but it's not playing any records. Still, a voice comes through and says . . .

118. Bored in class one day, you shut your eyes, only to find that you can hear dozens of voices in your head. You realize that you can listen to the inner voices of your classmates, your teacher, and anyone else around you. How do you convince a friend of your new powers?

119. You discover that you have the power to make any animal speak—all you have to do is talk to them first. Where do you start?

120. **CONTINUE THE STORY:** I'm swimming in the ocean with my friends, enjoying summer vacation. Something slippery grazes my feet. When I look underwater, a mermaid stares back at me. Before I can scream, she pulls me down to a cave where a large pocket of air helps me breathe, and . . .

MEMOIR & AUTOBIOGRAPHY

The Story of You

Every person has a story to tell—including you! Some stories involve adventure, while others involve everyday moments that shape who we are. **Memoirs and autobiographies** allow writers to capture real-life experiences for others to read. Have you ever told a funny or exciting story about something that happened to you? Or maybe you remembered when you got lost or made a new friend. That's what memoirs are all about.

Some of the most memorable books ever written are memoirs and autobiographies. From **inspiring journeys** to **humorous childhood memories**, these stories offer insight into different lives, perspectives, and histories. A memoir is a true story about a special moment or experience

in someone's life. It could be about a challenge or an unforgettable day. On the other hand, an autobiography tells the whole story of a person's life. Both allow writers to share their thoughts, feelings, and memories, bringing real-life moments to life on the page.

Famous people, explorers, athletes, and even kids have written about their lives. But guess what? You don't have to be famous to write a great story—your life is already full of interesting moments, **big or small**, that are worth telling.

In this chapter, you'll explore fun prompts to help you remember, reflect, and write about your own experiences. So, grab a notebook and get ready to tell the most exciting story of all—yours!

WRITING TIPS

- Focus on your feelings at the time, not just the facts of what happened. This immerses you in the memory and encourages your readers to engage with you.
- Think about a theme or topic that you can center your story around, such as friendship, a challenging lesson, or discovering your bravery.
- Use all five senses to bring the story to life and expand on it. This will help you relive the experience and gather more descriptive information.

- Remember to use metaphors and similes to make the writing more interesting. Show the reader, don't tell them, as much as you can.

- Focus on a few short memories first before building into a longer piece of writing. You will find that you have lots of different nuggets that can branch off into larger stories.

MEMOIR PROMPTS

Put five minutes on the clock. Ready. Set. Write!

121. Have you ever been lost? Whether you were in a somewhat familiar place, like your neighborhood, or a brand-new environment, how did that experience feel? What did you do? Describe the feelings you had and the decisions you made.

122. Describe a special space that you like to visit or explore. This space can be one that you created, like a fort, or perhaps your local library or lake. What makes it special to you? What smells, sights, or sounds consistently remind you of this space?

123. **CONTINUE THE STORY:** The last time I went out to dinner with my family, it was fun because we were celebrating . . .

124. When was the last time you were brave? Maybe you had to do something that made you nervous or scared, but you did it anyway! What did it feel like before and after?

TWIST: Now write about a time when you weren't brave.

125. When was the last time you were surprised? It could be something big, like a surprise party, or something small, like receiving a random act of kindness. How did that experience feel?

126. **CONTINUE THE STORY:** It's the first day of school, and I feel . . .

127. Have you ever experienced déjà vu? It's when a new experience feels familiar to you or like something you've already experienced. What did that feel like?

128. **CONTINUE THE STORY:** The most exciting day I've ever had was . . .

TWIST: What was the worst day you ever had?

129. What's your first memory? Do you have a memory of being a toddler, sitting in someone's lap, or being carried? Describe the memory as clearly as possible.

TWIST: Now write about your parents' first memory of meeting you!

130. If you have a sibling, write about a time when you got into some fun trouble together. If you don't have a sibling, try to remember an experience with a close friend instead.

TWIST: Even though you got "in trouble," would you do it again? Why or why not?

131. What's the most challenging conversation you've ever had with a friend or family member? Write about the experience and how it felt leading up to it versus afterward.

132. **CONTINUE THE STORY:** The last time I was excited about something was because . . .

133. Have you ever read a book that pulled you so deeply into the story that you felt like you were a part of its world? Describe the story and why it got you so invested.

134. Think of everything you've experienced in life so far. If you were to make a scrapbook of your entire life, what would go in it? What photographs or objects would you include?

135. **CONTINUE THE STORY:** I used to be afraid of . . . Explain in detail what it was and how you overcame it.

136. Have you ever had to speak up or stand up for someone or help another person out? Write about what happened and what it felt like.

137. If you had the power to change one rule at school, which one would you choose? Why would you change this rule? Has it been especially challenging to follow? Would changing this rule enhance the whole student body?

TWIST: If you were to write a letter to the principal convincing them to get rid of it, what would it say?

138. Think of a time when you've had a fun experience with an animal. Was it your pet or someone else's? Maybe it was a deer in the woods. Describe the experience in detail.

139. CONTINUE THE STORY: Being part of a team is . . .

140. Has there ever been a time when you couldn't stop laughing? It might have been a joke or even just a funny friend being themself. What happened that was so hilarious?

TWIST: Now write about a time when you couldn't stop crying.

141. Reflect on a time when you made a friend or had a connection with someone and then never really saw them again. Was it someone you met at summer camp or at the library? How did you connect, and how does it feel to reflect on them?

142. **CONTINUE THE STORY:** When I was four, my favorite toy was . . .

TWIST: What made it so important to you?

143. Try to remember the first time you stayed away from home. It could have been your first sleepover, a summer camp, or visiting with relatives. What made it so scary, and how did it feel afterward?

144. **CONTINUE THE STORY:** The last time I was sad . . .

TWIST: If you could relive that experience again, would you do anything different?

145. When was the last time you worked hard to solve a puzzle or a riddle? Was it in class or outside of school? What made the situation challenging, and how did it feel when you accomplished it?

TWIST: What about the last time you gave up? Explain what happened and why you stopped trying.

146. Have you ever investigated something on your own? Perhaps you discovered a family mystery or helped your friend find something that was missing. Describe gathering the clues and how you put them together.

147. Do you remember the first story you ever wrote? Maybe it was your first piece of creative writing that you remember. What was it about, and how did creating something new from your imagination make you feel?

148. What's the best advice you've ever received? It could have been from a long time ago or a more recent experience, from your favorite aunt or coach. What was the advice, and why has it stayed with you?

149. **CONTINUE THE STORY:** My favorite subject in school is ______ because I like . . .

150. What's a special tradition you have with your parents? Is it a recurring movie night, weekend adventure, or something else? Describe what makes it so important to you.

Conclusion

As you reach the end of this book, remember: Your writing journey is just beginning! Whether you're crafting a thrilling mystery, a fantastical adventure, a heartfelt memoir, or an out-of-this-world sci-fi tale, your words can bring stories to life. Keep exploring new ideas and asking, "What if?"

Don't be afraid to let your imagination run wild. Most importantly, have fun! Every great writer started just like you, with a love for stories and an excitement to create. So, grab your pen, open your notebook, and keep writing.

The world is waiting to hear from you!

Resources

BOOKS TO INSPIRE YOU IN EVERY GENRE

FICTION

Tales of a Fourth Grade Nothing by Judy Blume

MYSTERY

Enola Holmes Mysteries series by Nancy Springer

SCI-FI

The Wild Robot by Peter Brown

FANTASY/ADVENTURE

Eragon by Christopher Paolini

MEMOIR

Anne Frank: The Diary of a Young Girl by Anne Frank

PODCASTS ABOUT WRITING FOR KIDS

The Story Seeds Podcast

Young Writers

Kids Ask Authors

Acknowledgments

Writing this book would not have been possible without the support and encouragement of so many wonderful people. First, a huge thank-you to the Muse Writers Center—a fantastic resource for young writers and a space where creativity thrives. To my writing professors at the University of Pennsylvania and Boston University's School of Communication, your guidance and wisdom have shaped the writer and teacher I am today. To my incredible writing workshop group, the Write Story Creative Writing Community, thank you for always showing up with open minds, ready to inspire and be inspired. Your enthusiasm for storytelling is contagious. And finally, to every young writer who picks up this book, keep dreaming, keep creating, and most importantly, keep writing. Your stories matter!

About the Author

Chevahn Brown has been a storyteller since childhood. While attending the Winsor School, she self-published young adult dramas. She honed her craft at the University of Pennsylvania, where she studied creative writing. She later earned her MFA in screenwriting for film and television from Boston University's School of Communication. Her thriller television pilot, *Kane*, placed in the international Final Draft Big Break Contest, launching her into the world of storytelling and higher education.

As an adjunct professor of screenwriting, Chevahn has taught at Emerson College, Lesley University, and Boston University. She also runs the Write Story Editorial, a narrative consulting company where she coaches writers and hosts a story development group. Passionate about nurturing young writers, she leads creative writing workshops at the Muse Writers Center. Her stories often explore alternate realities, the multiverse, and the profound complexities of fate, love, and free will.

She resides in Boston with her two bright and curious children.

NOTES

Hi, parents and caregivers,

We hope your child enjoyed *5-Minute Writing Prompts for Kids*. If you have any questions or concerns about this book, or have received a damaged copy, please contact customerservice@penguinrandomhouse.com. We're here and happy to help.

Also, please consider writing a review on your favorite retailer's website to let others know what you and your child thought of the book!

Sincerely,

The Zeitgeist Team